A New True Book

DRUG ABUSE

By Dennis Fradin

Consultant: Barbara Weigand, Certified
Associate Addiction Counselor,
Parkside Lodge of Mundelein,
Illinois

CHILDRENS PRESS ®

CHICAGO

Demonstrators wear "Just say no" T-shirts at an anti-drug rally in Harpers Ferry, West Virginia

PHOTO CREDITS

© Cameramann International, Ltd.—7, 13 (left)
© Colman Communications—11 (left), 16 (right), 22, 25, 28, 32, 34, 36, 37

Journalism Services, Inc.:
© Richard Derk—18 (left)
© Paul F. Gero—Cover, 2, 40 (right)
© Joe Jacobson—8 (2 photos), 35 (top)
© Ingrid Johnsson—21 (right)
© Mike Kidulich—10
© Harvey Moshman—39
© John Patsch—16 (left)
© SIU—27
© SIU, Paul Fry—4
© Dennis Trowbridge—18 (right)
© Scott Wanner—14 (2 photos)

Medichrome:
© Brian Ashley White—45

Root Resources:
© Lisa Ebright—31, 35 (bottom left), 40 (left)
© Ray Hillstrom—12, 21 (left), 23 (left)
© MacDonald Photography—6
© David Stoecklein—11 (right), 35 (bottom right)

American Cancer Society—13 (right)

Library of Congress Cataloging-in-Publication Data

Fradin, Dennis B.
    Drug Abuse / by Dennis B. Fradin.
            p.   cm. — (A New true book)
    Includes index.
    Summary: Defines drugs, discusses the different types and their effects on people when used or abused, and suggests ways of preventing or counteracting drug abuse.
    ISBN 0-516-01212-6
    1. Drug abuse—United States—Juvenile literature.   2. Drug abuse—United States—Prevention—Juvenile literature.   [1. Drugs.   2. Drug abuse.]   I. Title.
HV5825.F73   1988   87-33789
362.2'9'0973—dc19   CIP
                                                    AC

For their help, the author thanks:

Caroline Gibbons, Midwest Center for Chemical Dependency, Chicago, Illinois

Kate Mahoney, Program Director, Comprehensive Drug Treatment Program, Evanston, Illinois

TABLE OF CONTENTS

A pharmacist prepares drugs in a hospital pharmacy.

WHAT ARE DRUGS?

Drugs are substances that cause changes in the body and the mind. Doctors prescribe certain drugs to help sick people. For example, drugs are used to cure people of pneumonia. Drugs are used to reduce high blood pressure. The drugs prescribed by doctors are called medicines.

Pharmacists cannot give out drugs without
a prescription from a doctor.

Medicines are obtained
at pharmacies, which are
also called drug stores.
Because doctors prescribe
drugs to help sick people,
drugs can do a great deal
of good.

But drugs can also do a
great deal of harm. They
can cause people to lose

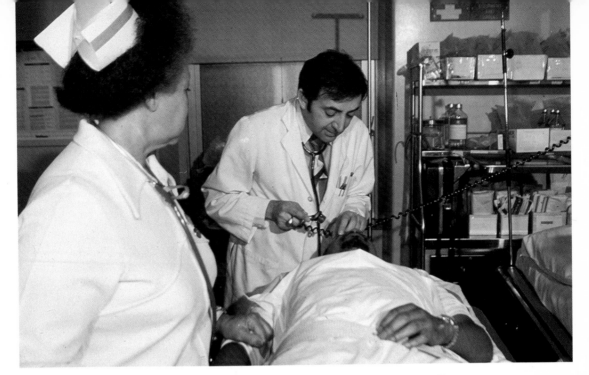

Emergency room care

their health, jobs, homes,
and everyone and
everything they love. Drugs
can land people in the
hospital—and even in the
graveyard. People who
take drugs that harm them
are called drug abusers.

7

Although illegal,
some people grow
marijuana (above) and
smoke handmade
cigarettes.

WHAT DRUGS DO PEOPLE ABUSE?

Many drugs that people abuse are against the law. They are not prescribed by doctors. Neither are they sold at pharmacies. People often buy these illegal drugs from drug dealers, whose only goal is to make money.

One drug that is often used illegally is called marijuana. Marijuana is a

part of the hemp plant
that is usually smoked. But
some people mix it with
food and eat it. Marijuana
can be very bad for
people. Other illegal drugs
can do even more harm.
Among the most harmful
of these illegal drugs are
heroin, LSD, and cocaine.

Cocaine

Alcohol is a drug. It causes changes in the body and mind.

Legal drugs can also be
abused. For example,
adults can legally drink
beer, wine, and other
drinks that contain the
drug alcohol. Alcohol is
the number one drug of
abuse in the United States.

Each year thousands of

Driving while under the influence of alcohol is dangerous.

people who are drunk on
alcohol die in car crashes
or destroy their lives in
other ways.

Tobacco is legal. But it
contains harmful drugs,
such as nicotine, that
cause many thousands of

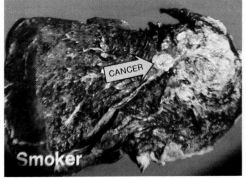

Smoking is harmful to the body. It destroyed the healthy tissue of the lung shown above.

people to die of lung cancer and other diseases each year.

Even the medicines prescribed by doctors can be abused. Some patients, for example, ignore the

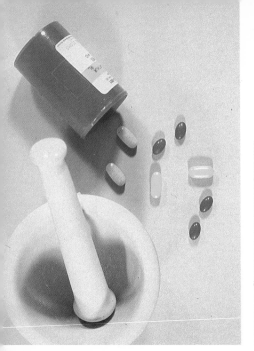

John Doe
Take one tablet four times a
day for 10 days.
Penicillin VK 250mg #40
11/27/87 lss

CAUTION: Federal law prohibits the transfer of this drug to any person other than the patient for whom it was prescribed.

A prescription drug (left) and specific directions for its use (right)

directions on the medicine container. Instead of taking one pill, they take many pills at a time. Abusing prescription drugs can be as harmful as taking illegal drugs such as heroin or cocaine.

WHY DO PEOPLE USE DRUGS?

Although they know that drugs are dangerous, many people continue to use them. For example, even though the dangers of cigarettes and alcohol are well known, many people smoke and drink every day. People who use heroin and cocaine know that these drugs can kill them. But they continue to

Drugs cause problems. They do not make problems go away.

use them. If these drugs
are so dangerous, why do
people abuse them?

Everyone has problems.
It is not always easy to
get along with one's
parents, friends, or
teachers. It can be hard to
get good grades, do well

at sports, or earn enough
money. Some people find
it difficult to feel happy or
calm.

Some people think that
drugs can help them
escape their problems—for
a while. Drugs can
temporarily make a sad
person feel happy, a
nervous person feel calm,
or a bored person feel
excited. Most people who
use drugs do so for these

Using drugs can seriously hurt the drug users' ability to relate to their friends and family. It also affects their ability to do well in school or on the job.

good feelings. But the good feelings last only a short time.

However, some of the people who start using drugs don't have problems. Some of them feel fine to start with, but think that drugs will help them feel even better. Others are curious about drugs and want to see what they are like. Still others take drugs because their friends do and they don't want to feel different or left out.

Whatever their reasons, all drug users have a problem that can ruin their lives and even kill them. Their problem can also ruin the lives of those who love them.

HOW DRUGS HARM AND KILL PEOPLE

People can become addicted to certain drugs. Addicts crave drugs the way most of us want food when we are hungry. This strong need for the drug may not just be in the person's mind. The addict's body may come to crave the drug too. Without the drug the addict may suffer withdrawal sickness.

Withdrawal sickness can involve chills, sweating, vomiting, and other problems. To avoid feeling this way, addicts keep taking the drug. This is how many people become "hooked" on drugs and find it hard to stop taking them.

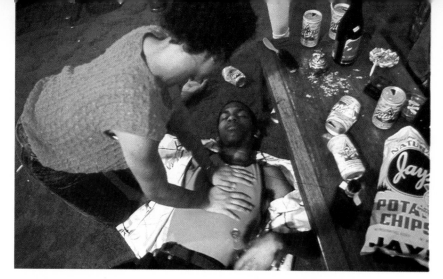

Some people never recover from a drug overdose.

People's bodies can get used to drugs. This is called building up tolerance. To have an effect, the drug must be taken in larger and larger amounts.

When larger amounts of drugs are taken, there is great danger of an overdose. This occurs when a person takes more of a drug than the body can handle. An overdose can cause brain damage and even death.

People also tend to do dangerous things while under the influence of drugs. Drug users have a large number of car crashes and other accidents.

Some drugs even give people the idea that their friends and families are out to "get" them. These users may get into fights with the people who love them the most.

In addition, many drug users cannot hold down jobs because drugs have harmed their bodies and minds. Since drugs are expensive, many users turn to stealing. They ruin their lives not only by taking

Drug addict
injecting
a drug

drugs, but also by becoming criminals.

Some drugs, such as heroin, can be taken by injecting them into veins. Addicts who inject drugs often share needles. The needles become filled with germs, which can cause the deadly disease AIDS and other illnesses.

WHO ABUSES DRUGS?

Many people think that only teenagers and young adults abuse drugs. It is true that too many young people do abuse drugs. But drug addicts can be found in every age group, from newborns to the elderly.

Perhaps you are wondering how a newborn baby can be a drug addict. When a pregnant

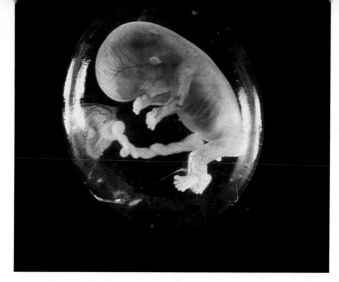

A human fetus

woman takes drugs, the fetus inside her can also become addicted to the drugs. Doctors use special medicines and treatments to help such babies conquer their addiction.

Drug addicts can be rich or poor. They can live in big cities or in small towns. Addicts are found among

people of every occupation.
   When a famous person
dies or enters the hospital
due to drug abuse, it may
make the headlines. But
every day the same thing
happens to thousands of
less-famous people all
over the world.

CAN DRUG ADDICTS BE HELPED?

Drug addicts can be helped. Doctors and other experts on drug addiction provide this help. They use several methods, depending on the type of drug involved and the individual needs of the patient.

Many experts believe that the best way to overcome drug addiction is to take away the drug completely. This is known as going "cold turkey." The patient enters a hospital or treatment center and is not allowed to take any drugs.

Many people who have abused drugs must learn how to live without their drug. After leaving the hospital or treatment center they are not ready

Those who have abused drugs need the guidance and support of professional people to help them overcome their problem.

to return home. There are special places where they can get more help before returning home. One such place is the halfway house. The staff of the halfway house helps the person get started on a drug-free life.

Teens at an Alcoholics Anonymous meeting

There are also support groups to help recovering addicts and their families. Two such groups are Alcoholics Anonymous and Cocaine Anonymous. People attend meetings of these groups to discuss their problems with other addicts.

SAYING NO TO DRUGS

Unfortunately, many people who have been drug addicts stop taking drugs for only a while. Perhaps they stay drug-free for a month or even a year. But a large number of them return to drugs. This happens for several reasons.

For one thing, it isn't easy for former addicts to stay away from drugs or

alcohol. After leaving a
treatment center, many
people return to the same
conditions and problems
that led them to use drugs
before. They go back to
the same neighborhood,
which may have many
drug pushers. They return
to the same friends, who

Drug addiction is common in all neighborhoods and in all life-styles. The expensive habit makes some people steal and even kill.

Say no to alcohol.

may again offer them
drugs. Former drug addicts
must work very hard to
keep themselves drug-free.

The best way for a
person to handle drugs is
to avoid using them in the
first place. And it isn't
always easy to say no to
drugs.

Do you decide, or do they? That is the question every person must decide for himself or herself.

Put yourself in this situation. You are with some friends. They are smoking marijuana, drinking alcohol, or taking pills. They offer you some. They tell you it cannot harm you. What do you do?

You might be tempted to try the drugs for several reasons. You might be curious about the drugs. Or, you might be worried that your friends will think you're a "wimp" if you refuse.

If you're smart, you'll say NO. You'll say NO because drugs—including marijuana and alcohol—can harm your body and your mind.

You'll say NO because
people can get "hooked"
on drugs. You'll say NO
because drugs have sent
millions of people to the
hospital and to the
graveyard.

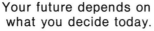

Your future depends on
what you decide today.

The decision not to use
drugs is one big way that
you can help yourself and
perhaps even save your
own life.

Decide that you will
never use drugs. Then
stick to your decision. It's
your life—live it.

TEN ABUSED DRUGS

Drug	Nicknames	Comments*
alcohol	booze, sauce, juice	breaks down people's health in many ways, destroys families, and causes thousands of accidental deaths each year
amphetamine	speed, upper, pep pill	speeds up brain activity; can make people violent and cause brain damage
barbiturate	downer, goofball	slows down parts of the brain and body; when taken in too large a quantity, can put the brain to sleep completely, killing the person
cocaine	coke, snow, flake	makes people "high," but leaves user feeling very depressed afterwards; can cause mental problems and ruin the breathing organs
heroin	smack, junk, H, boy	a highly addictive drug that often leads to an overdose
LSD (lysergic acid diethylamide)	acid	causes people to hallucinate (think they experience things that aren't there); can badly harm the mind
marijuana	pot, grass, weed, tea	puts people in a dreamy state called a "high"; can cause panic attacks and a variety of health and learning problems
methaqualone	quaaludes, ludes	a drug that is often abused; can lead to convulsions, heart failure, and comas
PCP (phencyclidine)	angel dust	can cause very violent behavior, comas, and death
tranquilizer	downer	when prescribed by doctors, tranquilizers can calm nervous people, but many people abuse tranquilizers by taking too many of them; very dangerous when taken with alcohol

* All of these drugs can cause death

FIVE DRUG ABUSERS

The following stories do not use real names. The author wrote these stories after talking to workers at several drug treatment centers. The stories are true in that thousands of similar cases exist for each one.

ROBERT

When Robert was twelve, he was miserable. He was doing badly in school. He was sad about his parents' divorce. When Robert was offered marijuana by some friends, he accepted. Soon he was using the drug as often as he could. Robert is thirteen now, and he smokes a lot of marijuana and also drinks alcohol. First he smokes the marijuana. Then when he starts coming "down" from the marijuana, he drinks alcohol to feel better again. He usually sneaks the alcohol from his mother, who drinks too much herself. To buy marijuana, Robert has stolen money from his mother's purse several times, but she has not caught him yet. He is drunk or high often and finds that he cannot concentrate very well, even when he wants to. Robert is so far behind in school that he hates going there, so he plays hooky at least once or twice a week.

KEVIN

Kevin is a sixteen-year-old sophomore who, until recently, got drunk most weekends. He bragged to his friends that he could "hold his liquor" without getting sick. He often got into fights when he was drunk. On Monday mornings when he came to school with bruises and black eyes, he told everyone that he "beat up the other guy real bad." If anyone told Kevin's parents that he had a drinking problem, they would say, "A little beer won't hurt him. We did the same thing when we were his age." Recently Kevin was driving drunk when he misjudged a turn and smashed his car into a tree, killing his girlfriend who had been sitting beside him. Kevin stopped drinking when he got out of the hospital. But he feels so bad about his girlfriend that he has started drinking again.

LAURA

Eighteen-year-old Laura always did everything well. She earned great grades. She was offered drugs in high school, but always said no. Then at a graduation party some of her friends were smoking marijuana. Laura decided to try it—just once. She didn't know it, but someone had sprinkled angel dust on her marijuana. The drugs made Laura act crazy. Thinking she could fly, she jumped out of a window and broke both legs.

ART

Art was a thirty-five-year-old lawyer who worked long hours. One day a friend gave him some cocaine, explaining that it would help him work faster and better. Soon Art was snorting cocaine several times a day. The problem was that, after the good feeling wore off, Art would be left with a very sad feeling. He had to keep taking more and more cocaine to drive away the sad feelings. Also, the cocaine was very expensive. To pay for it, Art took money from his family. His wife begged him to go for help, but Art became very abusive to her and the children. He said they were all against him. Eventually the only thing Art seemed to love was cocaine. One day he realized that he had ruined his life and the lives of everyone around him. Art killed himself.

EDITH

Edith is a seventy-year-old woman who began having trouble sleeping after her husband's death. The sleeping pills she got from a doctor helped at first, but Edith soon found that she had to take

Drugs can kill. Say no to all drugs.

more and more pills to fall asleep. Edith has
several doctors and managed to get sleeping pills
from all of them. The big problem was that the
pills left her "in a fog." Edith's children did not
realize she was abusing the pills. They thought she
was losing her memory due to old age. While "in a
fog," Edith fell and broke her hip. The people at the
hospital found out about her drug abuse. They will
try to help her overcome her problem.

45

WORDS YOU SHOULD KNOW

alcohol (drinking alcohol) (AL • kuh • hawl) — a legal drug that damages people's organs and contributes to thousands of accidents each year

angel dust (AYN • juhl DUHST) — a nickname for PCP, an illegal drug that causes very violent behavior, comas, and death

cigarettes (sig • uh • RETZ) — legal substances that contain drugs which cause many thousands of cancer deaths each year

cocaine (koh • KAYN) — a highly dangerous, illegal drug that provides a strong "high" but which can be very deadly

"cold turkey" (KOHLD TUR • kee) — the sudden stopping of drug abuse

"dope" (DOHP) — a nickname for drugs; also, people who abuse drugs are dopes

downers (DOW • nerz) — a nickname for drugs that relax people and help them go to sleep

drug abusers (DRUHG uh • BYOOZ • erz) — people who take drugs that can harm them

drug addicts (DRUHG AD • ikts) — people who are so dependent on drugs that they feel they cannot stop taking them

drug dealers (DRUG DEEL • erz) — or drug pushers; people who sell drugs illegally

drugs (DRUGZ) — substances that cause changes in the body and the mind

heroin (HEHR • oh • win) — a very dangerous, illegal drug that is often injected

"high" (HY) — a state of mind experienced by many drug users; some people who get "high" feel happy or peaceful, but others feel dizzy and confused

LSD—a very dangerous, illegal drug that causes people to see, feel, smell, taste, or hear things that aren't there

marijuana(MAIR • ih • wahn • nuh)—a dangerous drug that is smoked or eaten. It is illegal in many countries.

medicines(MED • ih • sinz)—drugs prescribed by doctors

overdose(OH • ver • dohs)—the taking of an especially dangerous amount of a drug

pharmacies(FAHR • muh • seez)—places where people obtain medicines prescribed by doctors

prescription(pri • SKRIP • shuhn)—an order for a medicine made by a doctor

tolerance(TAHL • uh • ruhnss)—the state in which people need larger and larger doses of a drug because their bodies have become used to the drug

tranquilizers(TRAN • kwuh • lyz • erz)—drugs that doctors use to calm people; many people abuse them

"uppers"(UHP • erz)—a nickname for drugs that speed up brain activities, making people more excited and alert; one kind of "upper" is called "speed"

INDEX

About the Author

*Dennis Fradin attended Northwestern University on a partial
creative scholarship and graduated in 1967. His previous books
include the Young People's Stories of Our States series for
Childrens Press, and Bad Luck Tony for Prentice-Hall. In the True
book series Dennis has written about astronomy, farming, comets,
archaeology, movies, space colonies, the space lab, explorers, and
pioneers. He is married and the father of three children.*